Contents

A Note About These Stories

In 1946, the country of Korea became two separate nations. The new countries were North Korea (The People's Republic of Korea) and South Korea (The Republic of Korea). The capital city – the most important city – of North Korea is Pyong-yang. The capital city of South Korea is Seoul.

The beautiful lands of Korea are in Northeast Asia. In the north, Korea has a border with China. To the east of Korea is the Sea of Japan. The Yellow Sea is to the west. Korea has many high mountains. But most Koreans live on the coast, by the sea. Or they live on the green, flat land by the rivers. Many people are farmers or fishermen. The farmers grow crops of rice, millet, vegetables and fruit in their fields. The fishermen catch fish from the sea.

Rice is a very important crop in Korea. Koreans eat rice with meat or vegetables. Garlic – a vegetable with a strong smell – is often put into Korean food.

The weather in Korea is hot and wet in the summer. In the winter, it is cold and dry. By the sea, there are often bad storms. Then, there is a lot of rain and the wind blows very strongly.

Long ago, there were huge forests of trees in Korea. Oaks, maples, sandalwood trees, pines and laurels grew in these forests. Some of these trees are in the stories in this book. Pine trees are tall and they have thin green leaves on long branches. Laurel trees have shiny dark green leaves and many short branches. The wood and the leaves of the sandalwood tree has a strong, sweet smell. Wormwood is in two of the stories. Wormwood is a plant, not a tree. The plant has a very bitter taste.

Many animals lived in the forests of Korea. Bears and tigers are in these stories. Bears have sharp teeth, and they have long, sharp claws on their paws. They eat fruit, insects and meat. Bears sleep in caves in the winter. Tigers are very big, strong cats. They have yellow and black marks on their bodies. They also have sharp teeth and sharp claws. They eat meat.

Bears and tigers are very large animals. There are also some very small animals in these stories – mosquitoes and ants. They are insects. Mosquitoes have wings and they fly in the air. Ants walk on the ground. Ants live together in very large families.

Some of the stories in the book are about things which happened many thousands of years ago. At this time, many people believed in gods and spirits. The gods lived in Heaven. Some spirits lived in Heaven too. Other spirits lived in the water, in the ground, in trees and in animals.

Later, the Buddhist religion came to Korea. Buddhism began in India, but it came to Korea from China. Buddhist monks lived in temples. They thought and they prayed. The monks were also teachers.

Different people have ruled Korea at different times. Chinese people first came to Korea in 108 BC. They brought many new ideas and laws to Korea.

An old name for Korea was Choson. Choson – or the Land of Morning Calm – was ruled for hundreds of years by families of powerful people. These families were called dynasties. One of the most important dynasties was called the Choson Dynasty. It ruled Korea from 1392 to 1910 AD.

The dynasties ruled the whole country. But each province, or part of Korea, was governed by an official – the governor. Every government official had to pass examinations. Officials helped people with their problems and they made people obey the laws.

millet

wormwood

measuring scales

a pine tree

an ant

a tiger

a pearl

a sandalwood tree

a laurel tree

a snake

garlic

a mosquito

a bear

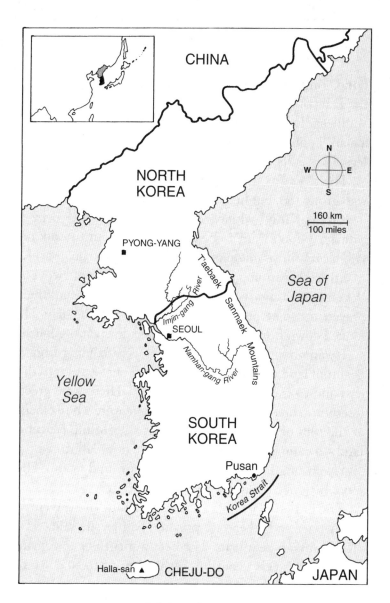

A Map of Korea

THE LAND OF MORNING CALM

Long, long ago, a tiger and a bear prayed to Hanunim, the King of Heaven.

'Please help me, Hanunim,' said the tiger. 'I want to be a man! I don't want to be an animal. I want to walk on two legs. Please, listen to my prayer!'

The tiger was strong and his voice was loud. The bear was strong too, but her voice was soft.

'Great King,' whispered the bear, 'I want to be a woman. I don't want to be an animal. I want to walk on two legs. Will you help me? Will you listen to my prayer?'

Prince Hwan-ung was the son of the King of Heaven. When animals prayed to his father, the prince heard their prayers too. The prince heard the tiger and the bear. He looked down from Heaven. He looked down at the Earth.

Hwang-ung smiled. The prayers were coming from a beautiful land with sea on three sides. There was sea to the east and to the south and to the west. There were green forests and blue lakes in the land. There were white clouds at the tops of tall mountains. It was a beautiful, peaceful land – a calm land. It was the land we now call Korea.

Hwan-ung looked at the land again and again. The more he looked at it, the more he liked it.

The prince spoke to his father, the King of Heaven.

'A tiger and a bear are praying, Father,' he said. 'The tiger wants to be a man. The bear wants to be a woman. Their land is very beautiful. Father, I want to go down to the Earth and rule that land. I want to be the king there.'

The King of Heaven smiled. Hwan-ung would be a good ruler.

'Go, my son,' Hanunim said. 'Take three thousand attendants with you. They will help you to rule the land.'

So Prince Hwan-ung left Heaven and he went down to the Earth. He took three thousand attendants and he went to the Tebeg Mountains in the north of the beautiful land. There, he rested by a sandalwood tree.

'I will build my city here,' Hwan-ung said. 'I will rule my new kingdom from this place.'

He called his wisest attendants and he spoke to them.

'You will have three important tasks in my kingdom,' he said. 'Your first task will be to govern the weather. You must take care of the wind and the rain and the clouds.

'Your second task will be to govern the crops,' the prince went on. 'You must take care of the rice and the beans and the corn which grow in the fields. And your third task will be to decide between good and evil. You must decide what is right, and you must decide what is wrong. You must make the laws.'

Then Prince Hwan-ung began to rule his land. And he ruled it well.

One day, when the prince was walking in his new kingdom, he saw the tiger and bear. They were praying near the sandalwood tree. He spoke to them.

'Bear, do you still want to be a woman?' he asked.

'Oh yes, Prince!' she replied.

'Tiger, do you still want to be a man?'

'Yes, Prince,' said the tiger.

Hwan-ung called one of his attendants.

'Bring some wormwood,' the prince said. 'And bring some garlic.'

The attendant brought the plants and Hwan-ung gave them to the tiger and the bear.

'Take this wormwood and this garlic to a cave,' he told the two animals. 'Stay in the cave for one hundred days. Eat nothing except these plants. Then, when one hundred days have passed, you will not be animals. Tiger, you will be a man. Bear, you will be a woman.'

The two animals were excited. They each took some wormwood and some garlic. Then they went to a dark cave in the side of a hill.

At first, both animals were patient. They sat quietly in the cave. But after a few days, the tiger started to walk round and round inside the cave. He hated the darkness. He wanted to be outside in the light. He wanted to run through the green forest. He wanted to swim in the lakes.

Soon, he had eaten all his wormwood and all his garlic. And soon, he was very hungry.

'I must have some meat!' the tiger cried. 'I must go into the forest and hunt for food!'

The tiger did not stay in the cave for one hundred days. After only fourteen days, he ran out of the cave and he did not return.

The bear was more patient than the tiger. She stayed in the dark cave. She ate a little of the wormwood and a little of the garlic every day. She became hungry. When

'Take this wormwood and this garlic to a cave,' Hwan-ung told the two animals. 'Stay in the cave for one hundred days.'

the tiger left, she became very lonely too. But the bear remembered Hwan-ung's words. And she obeyed him.

———

At last, one hundred days had passed. The bear came out of the cave. She looked down at her legs. She looked at her skin. She was no longer a bear. She was a beautiful young woman!

The bear-woman ran happily to the sandalwood tree. She thanked the King of Heaven. And then she prayed for a child.

'Hanunim, King of Heaven,' she whispered, 'I am your good servant. Please, give me a child. The child will be your servant too.'

Prince Hwan-ung saw the beautiful bear-woman and he heard her prayers. The prince fell in love with the bear-woman and he asked her to marry him.

'You and I will have a child,' said the prince. 'And our child will rule this land after me.'

Very soon, Hwan-ung and the bear-woman had a son. They called him Tan-gun, the Sandalwood Prince.

Tan-gun became a strong and brave young man. After some years, Hwan-ung made his son the king of the beautiful land. Then Hwan-ung returned to Heaven.

And so, King Tan-gun was the first Korean man. He called his beautiful kingdom 'Choson' – the Land of Morning Calm. He built a city at Pyong-yang, and he ruled wisely and well for a thousand years.

King Tan-gun was born more than four thousand years ago. Now, in October each year, Koreans have a holiday on Tan-gun's birthday. They call it National Foundation Day, or Tan-gun Day. Koreans say, 'Our history began when Tan-gun was born'.

THE SUN AND THE MOON

Once, a very long time ago, there was a poor woman who had two children. She was a widow – her husband was dead. The widow and her two children lived in a small house near a village. Between the widow's house and the village, there was a dark forest.

One day, the headman of the village gave the widow a basket of cakes.

'Today is a holiday,' he said. 'Take these cakes for your children.'

The widow thanked the headman and she started to walk home through the forest.

Suddenly, a tiger jumped onto the path in front of her.

'What's in that basket?' he asked.

'Only some cakes,' she said.

'I'm very, very hungry,' said the tiger. And he growled. 'I haven't eaten for two days. Give me one of your cakes!'

So the widow gave him a cake.

The tiger ate it quickly.

'That was good!' he said. 'Give me another cake!'

The tiger swallowed a second cake. Then he asked for another, and another, and another. Soon the basket was empty.

'You've eaten all my cakes,' the widow said sadly. And she walked on through the forest.

The tiger started to follow her.

'Where are you going?' he asked.

The tiger asked for another, and another, and another cake.
Soon the basket was empty.

'I'm going home,' she replied. 'I'm going to take care of my two children.'

'Children!' said the tiger. 'So, you have children! Are they soft and juicy?'

'No, no!' the widow said quickly. 'I was wrong. They are not children. They're both grown up!'

The tiger growled again. 'I'm very, very hungry,' he said. 'Large, grown-up people would be good. They would be very, very good.'

The widow turned. She was very frightened. The tiger's green eyes were bright and his white teeth were very sharp. He was licking his lips!

The widow started to run, but the tiger ran after her. He jumped onto her. He tore off her jacket. His great mouth opened. The widow saw his sharp teeth!

A moment later, the tiger had swallowed her.

The tiger licked his lips again. Then he put on the widow's jacket and he started to walk through the forest. He started to walk towards the widow's house.

———

At the widow's house, the two children – a boy and girl – waited for their mother. They waited and waited. Night came. The children were very worried. They looked through the windows and they looked out of the door. Everything was dark. They did not see anything. And they did not hear anything. They could hear nothing except the wind in the tall trees.

The children remembered their mother's words. 'Children,' she had said, 'always be careful at night. Lock the door. Close the shutters over the windows. The forest is dangerous. There are animals in the forest.'

So the children locked the door and they closed the wooden shutters over the windows. Then the frightened and hungry children tried to sleep.

———

The tiger walked along the path to the widow's house. He look around him. There was a very tall pine tree outside the wooden house. Next to the tree, there was a water-well. Drinking-water came from the well.

Quietly, the tiger tried to open the door at the front of the house. It was locked. Then he tried to open the windows. But the windows had shutters over them.

The tiger went to one of the windows at the side of the house. There was a small hole in the shutter. So the tiger whispered through the hole.

'Children, children!' he whispered. 'Please get the key and unlock the door!'

The two children were very surprised.

'Is that you, Mother?' asked the boy. 'Your voice is different.'

'Yes, I am your mother,' replied the tiger. 'My voice is different because I am ill. I have a cold. Please open the door quickly.'

The children looked through the hole in the shutter. They saw their mother's jacket. But they also saw the tiger's head and his cruel green eyes. They ran to the door. The boy turned the key and he quickly unlocked the door. Then the children ran out of the house and they climbed

The tiger whispered through the hole. 'Children, children!
Please get the key and unlock the door!'

up the tall pine tree by the well.

The tiger did not see them. He was still talking through the hole in the wooden shutter.

'I'm your mother,' he was saying. 'Open the door immediately!'

The children did not move.

'The tiger will get tired,' the boy whispered to his sister. 'He will soon go away.'

The tiger did not go away, but he did get tired. He had eaten a very big meal. So he lay down on the ground. Soon he was asleep.

_____

Early next morning, the tiger woke up.

'Where am I?' he asked himself. 'Why am I wearing this jacket? Ah, I remember. I am at the widow's house.'

He went to the door at the front of the house. Now, it was open!

'The children have escaped!' said the tiger. 'I must find them. I'm hungry again!'

The tiger took off the widow's jacket and he threw it on the ground. He was angry. He was angry because he was hungry.

But he was also very thirsty. So he ran to the well by the pine tree. He drank lots and lots of water.

While he drank, the tiger looked down into the well. The clear water of the well was a mirror. He could see the faces of the children. The children were in the tree above him but the tiger did not know that!

'The children are in the well,' he thought. 'That's

where they're hiding!'

The tiger growled. Then he put one of his huge paws down into the well. He tried to lift the children out of the water with his sharp claws.

The children looked down from the tree. They began to laugh.

'That stupid tiger almost fell into the well!' said the girl.

The tiger heard the children and he looked up.

'Oh, there you are,' he said. His voice was very soft. 'You are clever children. I will climb the tree. I will come up to you.'

'Yes, come up!' the boy replied. 'But first, you'll have to put some oil on the trunk of this tree. The oil will help you to climb up the trunk. There is some cooking-oil inside the house.'

The tiger quickly found the oil and he put some of it on the trunk of the tree. Then he tried to climb up the trunk. But he could not hold on to the trunk. His paws were covered with oil! Every time he tried to climb the tree, the tiger fell down.

The two children laughed.

'You're very unkind,' the tiger cried. 'I don't want to hurt you. I want to look at the forest from the top of the tree.'

The tiger started to weep. The children forgot about the danger. They wanted to help the tiger.

'There's an axe near the door of the house,' the boy said. 'It's very sharp. It will cut wood easily. You can cut some steps into the trunk. Then you'll be able to climb up into the tree.'

The tiger picked up the axe. He cut some steps into the trunk of the tree. Then he began to climb. But when he came close to the children, he started to growl loudly.

The children were sitting high up in the branches of the tree. They were very frightened. They looked up into the sky and they prayed.

'Hanunim, King of Heaven!' they cried. 'We are in great danger! Please help us!'

Hanunim heard the cries of the frightened children. Suddenly, a strong iron chain came down from Heaven. Quickly, the boy and the girl climbed up the chain. They climbed up to Heaven. Then the iron chain disappeared.

The tiger was angry. The children had escaped again! Could he follow them?

'Hanunim, King of Heaven,' the tiger prayed. 'I am the children's friend. I want to climb to Heaven too.'

Hanunim heard the tiger's prayer. Another chain came down from Heaven. But this chain was different. It was not made of strong iron. It was a silver chain. It was beautiful, but it was not strong. It was very weak.

The tiger was excited. Now he could climb up to Heaven. He could catch the children and eat them!

He held the end of the silver chain with one of his huge paws. Then he began to climb. But the tiger was very heavy and the chain was very weak. The chain broke, and the tiger fell back to the ground.

———

He held the end of the silver chain with one of his huge paws.
Then he began to climb.

The children were very happy in Heaven. They were not hungry and they were not frightened.

After some time, Hanunim called the children.

'Everyone who lives here has a task,' he said. 'And I have decided to give you your tasks now. You are both good children. You will do something to help the men and women on the Earth.

'You will be the Sun to light the day,' he told the boy.

'And you will be the Moon,' he told the girl. 'You will shine in the sky at night.'

'Oh, King of Heaven,' said the girl. 'I don't want to be alone at night. I don't want to be the Moon.'

Hanunim smiled at her. 'Very well,' he said. 'You will be the Sun and your brother will be the Moon.'

So the Sun shone each day, and the Moon lit the sky at night. And the people on the Earth looked up at them and smiled.

The Sun did not like people to look at her. So she shone more brightly. Now, you cannot look at the gold face of the Sun. It will hurt your eyes.

But you can look at the silver face of the Moon. And the Moon's silver face will look back at you!

THE GREAT FLOOD

Long ago, a spirit from Heaven loved a huge old laurel tree. The tree grew beside a river. The spirit often flew down from Heaven and sat next to the old tree. And the tree put his great branches around her. The tree loved the spirit and the spirit loved the tree.

One day, the spirit had a son. She lived with her child in the branches of the laurel tree. All year, the shiny green leaves of the old tree protected them. It protected them from the sun and it protected them from the rain.

The spirit lived happily in the tree and her baby grew into a strong boy. Then one day, she held her son's hands and she looked at him sadly.

'Dear son, my time here on the Earth is finished,' she said. 'I must return to Heaven. But the Great Laurel Tree will take care of you. Be a good boy. Always obey the Great Laurel Tree. He is your father.'

Then the spirit flew back to Heaven.

Soon after the spirit left the Earth, there was a great storm. Rain fell day after day. The water in the river rose higher and higher. There was a great flood. Soon, the water covered all the land. Many people died. They were drowned in the flood.

Day after day, the rain fell. The water was rising up the trunk of the Great Laurel Tree. One day, the tree spoke to the boy.

'My son, this rain will continue for many days,' the

24

tree said. 'I am weak now. Soon I will fall into the water. Climb up my trunk and hold on to my branches. Then, when I fall, you won't drown.'

So the boy climbed the trunk of the old tree and he held on to its branches. When the great tree fell, the boy did not fall into the water. He did not drown.

The flood carried the tree along and the boy sat on the trunk. The tree was his boat! He looked around him.

There was water everywhere. There was no land. There were no other trees. There was nothing! Nothing except water, and the top of a mountain, far away. The tree was travelling towards the mountain top. And still it rained!

Night came, and the boy went to sleep on the trunk of the great tree.

The next morning, the boy saw a family of small black ants. They were sitting on a stick of bamboo. The stick was moving through the water near the tree.

'This bamboo is very weak,' one of the ants said to the boy. 'If it breaks, we will fall into the water. We will drown! Please, let us climb onto your tree.'

The boy spoke to the laurel tree.

'Father,' he whispered. 'These ants are going to drown. Please let them climb onto your branches.'

'Very well,' the tree replied.

So the boy pulled the bamboo stick towards the Great Laurel Tree and the ants climbed onto the tree.

'Thank you very much,' they said.

The flood carried the tree along. The tree was still

moving towards the mountain top.

In the afternoon, some mosquitoes flew to the tree. They spoke to the boy.

'Please, oh please, let us rest on the leaves of your tree,' they said. 'There are no other trees anywhere, and we are very tired. We'll die if you don't help us.'

'Father,' the boy whispered to the tree. 'Please let these mosquitoes rest on your leaves.'

'Very well,' replied the tree.

So the mosquitoes sat on the shiny green leaves of the laurel tree.

'Thank you very much,' they said.

The Great Laurel Tree moved on over the flood of water. It was moving towards the mountain top. And the rain continue to fall. Soon it was evening again. Suddenly, the boy heard a cry.

'Help me! Help me! I'm drowning!'

The laurel tree's son looked down at the water. There was a boy holding on to a small piece of wood. The boy was the same age as himself.

'Father— ' the tree's son began.

'No!' said the Great Laurel Tree. 'This boy is bad. He will bring evil into the world.'

'But, Father, the boy will drown!' said the tree's son. 'Please, let him come with us.'

'No!' said the Great Laurel Tree. 'No! No!'

At that moment, the boy in the water screamed. Then he went down under the water.

'Father, I *must* help him,' the tree's son cried. Quickly,

The laurel tree's son looked down at the water.
There was a boy holding on to a small piece of wood.

he pulled the other boy out of the water. He pulled him onto the trunk of the Great Laurel Tree.

The tree said nothing.

The tree's son was unhappy. He was unhappy because he had not obeyed his father. But he was a kind young man. He could not let the other boy drown.

Night came. The tree, the two young men, the ants and the mosquitoes moved on together.

———

After many days, the Great Laurel Tree came to the mountain top. The mountain top was an island. There was water all around it.

It was evening. The two boys got off the tree and they stood on the ground. The ants walked quickly off the branches. They walked onto the ground too. The mosquitoes flew off their leaves and they flew up into the air.

The boys turned to look at the tree. But the Great Laurel Tree's task was finished. It had disappeared under the water.

'Father!' cried the laurel tree's son. 'Father, don't go! Don't leave me!'

'Come,' said the other boy. 'We must leave the tree. We must find food. And we must find shelter from the rain. Soon it will be dark.'

At that moment, the leader of the ants came up to the laurel tree's son. The ant spoke to him.

'You helped us,' the ant said. 'You saved our lives. If you ever need us, we will help you. We will always be near you.'

Then the leader of the mosquitoes flew up to the boy.

'And you helped *us*,' the mosquito said. 'If you ever need us, we will help you. We will never be far away.'

The laurel tree's son was happier. His father had gone, but now he had some new friends.

———

The two young men started to walk over the mountain. Soon, they saw a small house. The two young men were both very hungry.

'We will ask for some food at that house,' said the tree's son.

They knocked at the door of the house. An old woman opened the door and smiled at them.

'Come in, come in,' she said.

The boys sat by a fire and the old woman gave them some food. She asked them many questions. She talked about the flood. And she talked about her family.

'My daughter lives here with me,' the old woman said. 'And my husband had a daughter from his first marriage – my stepdaughter. She lives here too.

'My husband was a woodcutter,' the woman went on. 'When the rain started, he went down the mountain to sell wood. But he did not come back. He is dead – he has drowned. And everyone else has drowned too. We are the only people alive in the world! You must stay here with us.'

Then the old woman went into another room. Soon, she returned with two young women. Her stepdaughter was a pretty girl, but the old woman's own daughter was beautiful!

The laurel tree's son fell in love with the beautiful young woman immediately. And she fell in love with him. But the other young man fell in love with the old woman's beautiful daughter too!

The old woman did not say anything. She wanted both of her daughters to be married. But she wanted her own daughter to have the best husband.

'I will find out who is the cleverest boy,' she thought. 'He will marry my own daughter.'

The next morning, the rain stopped falling. There were wooden shutters on the old woman's house. The shutters had broken in the storm. The woman asked the two young men to mend the shutters. She watched them working.

Both young men worked hard. But the tree's son worked better than the other boy. He knew about wood. He could cut it easily. He could make things with wood.

'He is a clever young man,' the old woman thought.

The other young man became jealous of the laurel tree's son. He wanted to marry the widow's daughter himself. He had an idea. When the tree's son was in another room, he spoke to the old woman.

'My friend is very clever,' he said to the widow. 'He can do anything. Throw a bag of millet seeds down on the ground outside the house. My friend will be able to pick up all the seeds and put them back in the bag. He will be able to do this in two minutes.'

'Will he do that?' the old woman asked. She was very surprised. 'If he can pick up all the seeds, I will let him marry my daughter!' she said.

30

The laurel tree's son fell in love with the beautiful young woman immediately.

'If he does not *want* to marry your daughter, he will leave the seeds on the ground,' said the jealous young man.

So the widow called the laurel tree's son.

'Do you want to marry my daughter?' she asked him.

'Yes!' replied the laurel tree's son.

'Come with me,' she said. And she picked up a large bag of millet seeds.

The old woman and the young man went outside. The widow opened the bag. Thousands of seeds fell to the ground.

'Your friend has told me about you,' the widow said. 'You can do anything! If you can put all the seeds back in this bag, I will let you marry my daughter. But you must do it in two minutes! Bring the bag of millet into the house in two minutes.' Then she went inside again.

The laurel tree's son looked sadly at the seeds on the ground. It was an impossible task. He thought about the other boy – his friend. And he remembered his father's words. 'The boy is bad,' the old tree had said. Now he understood.

Suddenly, something bit the young man's leg. The young man looked down. And he saw a little black ant. It was one of the ants which had travelled on the tree.

'We will help you,' said the ant.

Hundreds and hundreds of ants ran to the seeds. Each ant picked up some millet and soon every seed was back in the bag. After two minutes, the laurel tree's son gave the bag of seeds to the widow.

Soon every seed was back in the bag.

When he saw what had happened, the other young man was very angry. The widow looked at him.

'Listen,' she said. 'I want both of you to marry. Each of you must marry one of my girls. But which young man will marry which girl? I have a plan. This is what I have decided.

'Tonight, when it is dark, one young man must go outside the house,' she went on. 'While he is outside, one of the girls will go to the small bedroom. And the other girl will go to the large bedroom. When I call, the young man who is outside must go to one of the rooms. He will marry the girl who is in that room. The other young man will marry the other girl. Do you agree to my plan?'

'Yes,' said the laurel tree's son.

'And do you agree?' the old woman said to the other young man.

'Yes, I agree,' he said. 'We both want to be married.'

Then the old woman called her stepdaughter. She gave the girl a millet seed.

'Go outside the house,' she said to the girl. 'When I call you again, come in and put the seed into one of my hands.'

When the girl had left the room, the widow spoke to the laurel tree's son.

'If the girl puts the seed into my left hand, you will make the decision tonight.'

Then she spoke to the other young man.

'If she puts the seed into my right hand, you will make the decision.'

The old woman held out her hands and she called her

stepdaughter. The girl came in to the room. She put the seed into the widow's left hand.

Late that night, the laurel tree's son left the house and he stood outside. He had to decide which room to go to. But he did not know how to decide!

The night was very dark. The moon was not shining. The young man could not see anything. But suddenly, he heard something.

He heard a mosquito flying near his head. It was one of the mosquitoes which had travelled on the Great Laurel Tree. It spoke to the young man.

'The beautiful daughter is in the small bedroom,' it said. 'She is in the small bedroom.' Then it flew away.

So the laurel tree's son tree went to the small bedroom. And there was the old woman's beautiful daughter! She smiled happily at him.

So the four young people were married. And soon, the flood waters disappeared. The land appeared again.

After a few years, the old woman died. Both of the young women had many children. But the two young men were not friends now. The laurel tree's son was good and kind. But the other young man was jealous and angry. He did evil things. The two families lived in different places.

We all come from these two families. They were the only people alive on the Earth after the great flood.

THE MAGIC SCALES

There was once a poor fisherman who lived in a village by the sea. Every day, he went on the sea in his boat. He went on the sea to catch fish. His wife sold the fish in the market. If the fisherman did not catch any fish, they had nothing to sell. And then they had no money for rice.

One day, the fisherman was sitting in his boat. He was unhappy. It was late afternoon, and he had not caught any fish. Many times, he threw his net into the sea. But each time, when he pulled it up again, it was empty. The sun was going down. Soon it would be dark and he would have to go home.

The fisherman moved his boat to a different place.

'I will not use my net,' he thought. 'I will use a fishing line.'

His fishing line was long and it had many hooks on it. He threw it into the sea and he waited.

Suddenly there was something on the fishing line! One of the hooks had caught a fish!

The fisherman pulled the fish out of the water. It was a big golden carp. It was the most beautiful carp that the fisherman had ever seen. The beautiful golden fish shone in the light of the evening sun.

The fisherman pulled the carp very slowly into the boat. Then, he carefully took the hook out of its mouth. The big carp looked at the fisherman and the man looked at the fish.

It was the most beautiful carp that the fisherman had ever seen.

'You are the most beautiful fish that I have ever seen,' said the fisherman. 'I cannot kill you.'

Yes, the fish was too beautiful to kill. Quickly and carefully, the fisherman put the carp back into the sea.

When he got home, the fisherman spoke to his wife.

'I did not catch any fish today,' he said.

———

The fisherman did not sleep well that night. The next morning, he got up very early and went to his boat. Suddenly, a strange young boy came out of the sea. The boy's skin was the colour of silver.

'Yesterday,' he said to the fisherman, 'you helped my master, the prince. You saved his life. He is the Great Golden Carp. Now the prince's father, the Dragon King, wants to thank you. The prince wants you to come with me. We will go to the Dragon King's kingdom under the sea.'

The boy turned round and he walked towards the water. Suddenly, there was a road through the sea! It was a long silver road.

The fisherman was very surprised. But he followed the boy along the road. The sea closed over their heads. Soon, the fisherman was in a wonderful world under the sea. He looked around him. There were strange trees and plants and fish of many colours.

At the end of the silver road there were two huge silver gates. The gates opened and the fisherman saw a beautiful palace. The palace was made of gold and silver and it was covered with pearls.

The young boy took the fisherman into the palace. They went through a golden door which was covered with pearls. Then they entered a huge room. And there, on a great golden chair, sat the Dragon King! He was wearing a crown of gold and silver and pearls and bright jewels. Near the king's chair, the fisherman saw some iron scales.

The fisherman bent his head forward. He bowed to the king.

'You saved the life of my dear son,' said the Dragon King. 'I thank you. Please stay here in my palace. You will be my guest.'

The fisherman could not think of anything to say. So he bowed again.

Soon, he was taken to a room with a bed of soft silk. He was given fine clothes to wear. He was given the best food and the best wine. Everywhere, he heard beautiful, soft music.

––––

At first, the fisherman was very happy. The golden carp-prince became his friend. There was no work to do. But then the fisherman started to think about his wife. He wanted to see her again. After a few days, he was very lonely. At last, he went to the Dragon King.

'Sir,' he said to the king, 'you have been very kind to me. But I want to go home.'

'Very well,' said the Dragon King. 'You will go home tomorrow. But you must take a gift with you. Take something from my underwater kingdom. What gift do you want? You can have anything. Come back tomorrow and

The Dragon King was wearing a crown of gold and silver and pearls and bright jewels.

tell me what you want.'

The carp-prince was sad. He liked the fisherman very much.

'When you return to the world of men,' said the carp-prince, 'take something useful with you. Ask my father for the iron scales which are near his golden chair. They are magic scales. They will give you anything that you want.'

So the next day, fisherman asked the Dragon King for the iron scales.

'No, I cannot give you the scales,' said the king. 'You can have anything except the scales.'

'But, Father,' said the prince, 'you must give the scales to the fisherman. He saved my life. Are the scales more important than my life?'

'No, they are not,' replied the Dragon King. And he gave the iron scales to the fisherman. Then he called the boy with the silver skin. The boy took the fisherman back to the world of men.

———

When he got home, the fisherman showed the magic scales to his wife. She was very angry.

'We don't need iron scales,' she said. 'We need fish to sell in the market. We have no money and we have no food.'

'The scales will give us food,' said the fisherman. 'You will be surprised.'

The fisherman spoke to the scales. He asked the scales for some food – and immediately, bowls of rice and meat and vegetables appeared. Then the fisherman's wife asked for some new clothes – and some fine new clothes appeared. Next, the fisherman asked for a new house – and the small wooden house became a strong stone house.

From that day, the fisherman and his wife had everything that they wanted. Soon, they became rich.

The people of the village were very surprised.

'Where did the fisherman and his wife get all this money?' they asked each other.

The wife of the headman of the village often went to the fisherman's new house. She wanted the fisherman's wife to be her friend. And she wanted to learn the secret of the fisherman's money.

One day, the headman's wife asked her new friend for some rice.

'There is no rice in our house,' said the headman's wife. 'My husband has given all our rice to poor people. Now we have none for ourselves.'

'I will give you as much rice as you want,' the fisherman's wife said.

She got the magic scales and she asked them for some rice. Immediately, two large bags of rice appeared. She gave the bags to the headman's wife.

'That is the secret,' thought headman's wife. 'The fisherman is rich because he has those magic scales. If I had those wonderful scales, I could be the richest woman in the land!'

Two days later, while the fisherman's wife was at the market, the magic scales were stolen.

'Who knew about the scales?' asked the fisherman that evening. He was very angry. 'Who knew the secret?'

'The headman's wife knew the secret,' his wife replied sadly. 'She saw the scales.'

The fisherman immediately went to the headman's house.

'Have you seen my iron scales?' the fisherman asked. 'Do you know where they are?'

'No, I have not seen them,' the headman said.

'And I do not know where your scales are,' said the headman's wife.

———

The fisherman and his wife had lost their magic scales. Soon, they were poor again. Every day, the fisherman went on the sea in his boat. Then the winter came. There were storms. The fisherman could not go on the sea. The weather was too bad. Soon, he and his wife did not have enough food.

The fisherman had a cat and a dog. The two animals were good friends. The cat and the dog were hungry too. The cat thought about the magic scales. She spoke to the dog.

'The scales gave us many good things,' said the cat. 'We must try to find the scales for the fisherman.'

The two animals started to look for the scales. They did not find them. But they saw something strange!

Every evening, the headman's wife came out of her house alone and she left village. When it was dark, she came back again, carrying two heavy bags.

43

One evening, the cat and the dog followed her. There was a river near the village. The woman walked to the river, then she got into a boat. She crossed the river and she went into a house on the other side. When it was dark, she came out of the house with two heavy bags. Then she went home again.

'The woman's brother lives in that house,' said the dog. 'The magic scales are in that house.'

So, the next evening, the cat and the dog followed the woman again. They followed her to the river. Then the dog got into the water and the cat got onto his back. The dog swam across the river, and the two animals followed the woman to her brother's house.

When the woman opened the door of the house, the cat quietly went inside. The cat followed the headman's wife to a small room. In the corner of the room, there was a big wooden box with a lock and a key. The woman unlocked the box and she lifted out the magic scales! She said some words, and immediately two bags of rice appeared.

When the woman left the house again, the cat ran out behind her. Then the cat called to a family of rats who lived behind the house.

'Help me,' the cat said. 'Help me or I'll eat you! Listen! You must go into that house. Then you must bite the lock of the big wooden box. Break the lock, then open the box. Inside it are some iron scales. Bring them to me!'

The cat had long white teeth and very sharp claws. The rats were frightened. They obeyed her immediately.

They went quickly into the house. They bit the wood around the lock of the big box. Soon, the box was open. The rats pulled the magic scales out of the box and they pulled the scales out of the house.

The cat picked up the scales in her mouth. She ran to the river. The dog was waiting for her. She jumped onto his back. Then the dog got into the river and he started to swim.

'Have you got the scales?' asked the dog.

The scales were in the cat's mouth, so she did not reply.

'Have you got the scales?' the dog asked again.

Still the cat did not reply.

The dog stopped swimming.

'Why don't you speak?' he asked angrily. 'Have you got the magic scales?'

'Yes, I have the— ' the cat began.

But when she opened her mouth, the scales fell into the river!

Now the cat was angry with the dog. She scratched his back with her sharp claws.

The dog swam quickly to the other side of the river. The cat jumped off his back and she walked away.

———

The next morning, the fisherman started to walk to his boat. But the dog pulled at the man's clothes. He pulled the fisherman to the river. Then the dog swam to the place where the cat had dropped the magic scales. He barked, again and again.

'Why are you making that terrible noise?' asked the

The rats pulled the magic scales out of the box.

fisherman. 'Have you found something in the river?'

The fisherman got his fishing net and he threw it into the river. When he pulled the net up again, the magic scales were in it!

'Good dog! Clever, clever dog!' the fisherman shouted happily.

When they got home, the fisherman asked the scales for some meat. And he gave the meat to the dog. But he did not give any meat to the cat.

'Good dog! Clever dog!' he said again. He did not say, 'Clever cat!'

The cat was jealous. Her eyes became green.

Now, all cats have green eyes. And now, cats and dogs hate each other. They always fight!

THE BUDDHIST MONK
AND HIS PUPIL

Long ago, in a province in the south of Korea, a village headman and his wife had one child – a boy. The headman was fifty years old when the child was born. So the child was very dear to the headman.

On the child's first birthday, the villagers made some special cakes of rice and wormwood. And the boy's parents gave him many gifts.

'One day, my son will be an important man,' his father said.

The boy grew up, but he became very spoilt. If he did not want to do something, he did not do it. If he could not have something, he cried. He behaved very badly. But the headman loved his son very much. He always forgave the boy and he spoilt him more and more.

Everyone in the village knew about the boy's bad behaviour.

'The boy must go to a teacher,' the villagers said.

But the headman would not send his son to a teacher. He did not want the child to leave his house.

———

Near the village, there was a large Buddhist temple. It was one of the largest temples in Korea. It was called the He-in Temple.

The head monk of this temple knew about the spoilt child. He went to see the boy's father.

The head monk was a very wise old man. So the headman listened to his words.

'Your son is now thirteen,' the monk began. 'You have not educated him – you have not sent him to a teacher. He cannot read or write. He behaves very badly.'

'My son is a good boy!' said the headman.

'He is not educated,' the monk said again. 'You are sixty-three years old. When you die, your son will become the head of your family. He will get married and have children of his own. But he knows nothing! What do you think will happen?'

The headman was silent.

'I know something else about your son,' the monk went on. 'I cannot tell you what I know. But I want you to send the boy to the He-in Temple. I will educate him there – he will be my pupil.'

The headman was unhappy.

'My son is very dear to me. I do not want to lose him,' he said. 'If I send him to the temple, will you let me come and see him?'

'No,' said the monk. 'The boy must live a different life. You must not come and see him. I will be his father now. Do you agree?'

Sadly, the headman agreed. He wrote his name on a paper – he signed it. The head monk was now the boy's father. He was going to educate the boy. The boy was going to be his pupil for many years.

———

The boy was very unhappy at the He-in Temple. His life at home had been easy. But his life at the temple was very difficult. The boy had to obey the monks. There were many rules. And when he did something wrong, the monks did not smile and forgive him. They punished him!

The headman's son wanted to go home.

'I hate this temple!' the boy cried. 'I want to leave!'

The monks did not listen to him. So the boy ran away. But the monks soon found him and they brought him back to the temple.

'My boy,' said the head monk, 'you must have a good education. Your father agrees with me.' And he gave his pupil the paper that his father had signed.

The monk had another paper. That paper had words about the boy on it too. But the monk did not give that paper to the headman's son.

At last, the boy understood. He had to stay at the He-in temple. He did not enjoy his life there, but he began to study his books.

The boy was a clever pupil. He learned to read and write quickly. Then there were many other things to learn.

———

The headman's son was going to become a government official. Everyone who wanted to be an official had to pass difficult examinations. After studying for a few years, the young man prepared to take his first examination.

He passed the examination easily. He did very well.

'Now you must prepare for the next examination,' said the head monk.

The monks brought him back to the temple.

Again the young man did very well. Soon, he became the governor of his province.

The headman was very proud of his son. But the young man still hated the monks who had educated him. When he became governor of the province, he made a decision. He spoke to one of his officials.

'I will visit the He-in Temple,' he said. 'I will close the temple. The monks will leave this province!'

———

The head monk stood at the gates of the He-in Temple. All the other monks stood behind him. They were waiting for the new governor and his officials.

'The new governor will close the temple,' said one of the monks sadly. 'He will send us away.'

But the head monk smiled. 'I will be happy to see the governor,' he said.

And when the new governor saw his old teacher, a strange thing happened. Suddenly, the young man did not hate the wise old monk any more. He loved him!

'If I hadn't been the old man's pupil, I wouldn't be the governor of this province today,' he thought. 'I'd be a very spoilt young man!'

So the governor bowed to all the monks.

'My dear friends,' he said. 'I will stay here at the He-in Temple tonight. I will be your guest.'

That evening, the head monk and the governor ate a meal together. Then, after the meal, the monk took his pupil to his own room. He went to a cupboard and he took out a piece of yellow paper. He gave the piece of

Suddenly, the young man did not hate the wise old monk any more. He loved him!

paper to the young man.

'I wrote this on the day of your birth,' said the old man.

On the paper was the story of the young man's life – his past and his future!

At the age of thirteen, he will go to the He-in Temple.
He will become the governor of his province.
He will do well and everyone will love him.
One day, he will become Governor of Pyong-an Province.

The young man read the paper and he smiled. 'Governor of Pyong-an? I do not believe it!' he said.

'One day, I will meet you in the city of Pyong-yang,' the head monk told him. 'I will go there because you will be the Governor of Pyong-an Province.'

'Pyong-an is the most important province in the north,' the young man said. 'I will never be Governor of Pyong-an!'

———

But the old man's words were true. Many years later, his pupil was Governor of Pyong-an Province, and the head monk went to meet him in the city of Pyong-yang.

That afternoon, the two men ate a meal together in the governor's house. But the head monk was very old now. And he was very tired after his long journey from the south.

'Let me rest in your bedroom, sir,' he said.

So the governor took the old man to his own bedroom.

'Please sleep here,' he said.

Late that evening, the head monk was still asleep in the governor's bed. The governor did not want to wake the old man. So he slept in another room. He slept very well.

But early the next morning, the governor heard a scream from one of his servants.

'Help! Help! Murder!' the servant shouted. 'The old monk is dead! Someone has murdered the old monk!'

The governor was very sad. He had loved his old teacher very much.

'Find the murderer!' he told his servants.

At last, the servants brought a frightened girl to the governor.

'Did you murder the old monk?' the governor asked the girl.

'Yes!' said the girl. 'But I was trying to kill you! Some people in this city are jealous of you. They told me to kill you. They gave me some money.

'The monk was in your bed,' the girl went on. 'I did not know that. It was dark. I killed the wrong man!'

Then the governor remembered the piece of yellow paper at the He-in Temple.

'The old monk knew about the future!' he said to himself. 'He knew what was going to happen. He knew everything! He knew about the murderer. He wanted to sleep in my bed. He wanted the murderer to kill him, not me!'

The governor wept.

'The monk was a good man,' he said. 'And I will be a good man too. I will be a good governor. I will take care of

The governor did not want to wake the old man.

my people.'

And that is what happened. The spoilt boy from a province in the south became one of the wisest governors in Korea!

Points for Understanding

THE LAND OF MORNING CALM

1 Who prayed to Hanunim, the King of Heaven?
2 What did they ask?
3 Who wanted to go down to the Earth?
4 What were the three important tasks?
5 What were garlic and wormwood?
6 Who stayed in the cave for fourteen days? What happened in the cave?
7 Who stayed in the cave for one hundred days? What happened in the cave?
8 Who was Tan-gun?
9 What happened to his father?
10 When do Koreans remember Tan-gun? Why do they remember him?

THE SUN AND THE MOON

1 What did the headman give the widow?
2 Who jumped onto the path in front of the widow?
3 Was the widow in danger? Find some words which give the reason for your answer.
4 The widow's two children were inside the house. They were waiting for their mother. Why didn't they open the door?
5 What question did the boy ask? What else did he say?
6 What answer did they hear?
7 Why did the children laugh when they were in the tree?
8 Hanunim heard two prayers.
   (a) Who prayed first? What happened next?
   (b) Who prayed second? What happened next?

9 What task did the boy have in Heaven?
10 What task did the girl have in Heaven?
11 Why does the Sun shine brightly?
12 Which can't you do – look at the face of the Sun, or look at the face of the Moon?

THE GREAT FLOOD

1 The spirit loved the laurel tree. Where had the spirit come from?
2 Where was the spirit's new home?
3 Why could she and her son live safely there?
4 What did the spirit tell her son?
5 What happened to the laurel tree and the boy when the flood came?
6 What were on the piece of bamboo?
7 What did they ask the boy?
8 What rested on the leaves of the tree?
9 Why didn't the tree want to help the boy who was in the water?
10 What happened when the Great Laurel Tree came to the mountain top?
11 Where was the old woman's husband, the woodcutter?
12 Which young man worked best? Why?
13 How did the laurel tree's son get all the millet seed into the bag again?
14 Why was the other young man jealous of the laurel tree's son?
15 What was going to happen if the stepdaughter put the millet seed into the widow's right hand?
16 How did the laurel tree's son decide which room to choose?
17 What was the difference between the two young men?

THE MAGIC SCALES

1 The poor fisherman had not caught any fish in his net. What did he do?
2 What did the fisherman catch then?
3 Why didn't the fisherman kill the fish?
4 Who did the fisherman see the next morning?
5 Where did this person take him?
6 What was made of gold and silver and covered with pearls?
7 Who did the fisherman meet?
8 What gift did the fisherman ask for?
9 What happened when the fisherman got home?
10 Who came to see the fisherman's wife?
11 What did this person want to find out?
12 What did this person ask for?
13 Which two animals wanted to help the fisherman?
14 What did they find out?
15 How did the animals open the wooden box in the house across the river?
16 What happened when the two animals started to cross the river again?
17 Who did the fisherman give some meat to? Why?
18 Which animal do you think was the cleverest?

THE BUDDHIST MONK AND HIS PUPIL

1 Why was the child very dear to the headman?
2 The boy grew up. What happened to him?
3 Why didn't the headman want to send his son to a teacher?
4 Who came from the He-in Temple?
5 What did the headman agree?
6 Why was the boy unhappy at the He-in Temple?

7 The boy ran away. What did the head monk give the boy?
8 The young man passed his examinations and he became the governor of his province. What decision did he make?
9 What happened when the pupil saw his old teacher? What did he do? What did he say?
10 What did the head monk give the governor that night?
11 Why was this important?
12 Why was the monk going to meet his pupil in the city of Pyong-yang?
13 The monk was tired after his long journey. What did he ask?
14 What did the governor do that night?
15 What happened to the old monk?
16 Who was brought by servants to the governor?
17 What did this person say?
18 What did the governor remember? What did he understand?

ELEMENTARY LEVEL

A Christmas Carol *by Charles Dickens*
Riders of the Purple Sage *by Zane Grey*
The Canterville Ghost and Other Stories *by Oscar Wilde*
Lady Portia's Revenge and Other Stories *by David Evans*
The Picture of Dorian Gray *by Oscar Wilde*
Treasure Island *by Robert Louis Stevenson*
Road to Nowhere *by John Milne*
The Black Cat *by John Milne*
The Red Pony *by John Steinbeck*
The Stranger *by Norman Whitney*
Tales of Horror *by Bram Stoker*
Frankenstein *by Mary Shelley*
Silver Blaze and Other Stories *by Sir Arthur Conan Doyle*
Tales of Ten Worlds *by Arthur C. Clarke*
The Boy Who Was Afraid *by Armstrong Sperry*
Room 13 and Other Stories *by M.R. James*
The Narrow Path *by Francis Selormey*
The Lord of Obama's Messenger and Other Stories
by Marguerite Siek
Why Ducks Sleep on One Leg and Other Stories *by Anne Ingram*
The Gift From the Gods and Other Stories *by Anne Ingram*
The Land of Morning Calm and Other Stories *by Anne Ingram*
Love Conquers Death and Other Stories *by Catherine Khoo and Marguerite Siek*
The Stone Lion and Other Stories *by Claire Breckon*
The Bride of Prince Mudan and Other Stories *by Celine C. Hu*

For further information on the full selection of Readers at all five levels in the series, please refer to the Heinemann Readers catalogue.

Heinemann English Language Teaching
A division of Reed Educational and Professional Publishing Ltd
Halley Court, Jordan Hill, Oxford OX2 8EJ

OXFORD MADRID FLORENCE ATHENS PRAGUE
SÃO PAULO MEXICO CITY CHICAGO PORTSMOUTH (NH)
TOKYO SINGAPORE KUALA LUMPUR MELBOURNE
AUCKLAND JOHANNESBURG IBADAN GABORONE

ISBN 0 435 27323 X

The stories *Tan'gun, the Bear Woman's Son, The Sun and the Moon,
The Great Flood, The Magic Measure* and *The Buddhist Monk and His Pupil*
were first published by Heinemann Southeast Asia
(a member of the Reed Elsevier plc group)
in *The Golden Legends of Korea* by Anne Ingram (1996)
© Anne Ingram 1996

These retold versions by Kathinerine Mattock for Heinemann Guided Readers
Text © Reed Educational and Professional Publishing Limited 1997
Design and illustration
© Reed Educational and Professional Publishing Limited 1997
First published 1997

Illustrated by Anthony Colbert
Illustrations and the map, pages 6 and 7, by John Gilkes
Typography by Sue Vaudin
Cover by Stewart Clough and Marketplace Design
Typeset in 11.5/14.5pt Goudy
Printed and bound in Malta by Interprint Limited

97   98   99 00   10   9   8   7   6   5   4   3   2   1